WITH HEART AND HANDS AND VOICES

Songs with Sign Language for Sunday School, Choir, and Worship

Compiled and Edited by Debra Tyree

Abingdon Press
Nashville

WITH HEART AND HANDS AND VOICES:
Songs with Sign Language for Sunday School, Choir, and Worship

This book is printed on acid-free, recycled paper.

ISBN 0-687-08992-1

Editor: Debra Tyree
Copy Editor: Julianne Eriksen
Design Manager: Linda Bryant
Sign Language Consultant: Annie Lloyd
Illustrations: Susan J. Harrison

00 01 02 03 04 05 06 07 08 09 — 10 9 8 7 6 5 4 3 2 1

MANUFACTURED IN THE UNITED STATES OF AMERICA

How to Use This Songbook

During the last several decades, the use of movement in worship and educational settings has become more and more prevalent. We have come to recognize not only the beauty of movement in worship, but also the many ways movement can enhance each person's understanding of worship and scripture. Sign language is a beautiful form of communication in itself. The combination of movement (sign language) and sound (song) enables God's children of all ages to join together in God's praise in a special way.

The sign language included with each song in this book is not intended to be a literal translation of the text. It is meant to enhance the text by providing the sign language to key words of each song. If you would like to learn more about sign language, most community colleges and adult education centers include sign language classes in their class catalogs. Many persons use sign language as a part of their daily life. Find out if there is someone in your church, school, community, or work who would be willing to come and help you as you learn to sign these songs.

Just as we have words that have different meanings in various areas of the United States or in other cultures, there are a wide variety of signs for the same word or phrase. This songbook uses American Sign Language as the primary illustration for the signs. If there is someone in your community who has expertise in sign language and knows of different signs for the same thing that are used more frequently in your community, simply make a note in your book. Also, a resource list at the end of the book includes several reference books you may want to consider.

The goal of this book is to allow people to add sign language to their worship and song in an act of praise. For some songs, an entire verse is signed; for others, you will sign only a stanza or repeating line. This information is clearly noted with each song. Several performance options are included. Additionally, each song has a short informative paragraph that can be used as an introduction. Persons always enjoy learning more about the story of the song and hymns. A short hymn story may be all you need to get someone interested and willing to try to learn to sing and sign. A list of hymn story reference books is included at the end of the book.

General Suggestions

1. Consider selecting one person to study the sign language in advance. Use this person as the primary leadership when teaching and leading the song.

2. Consider teaching the sign language to a choir, youth group, Sunday school class, or weekday school class a part of your curriculum. In addition to using the sign as part of your teaching time, have the group lead the congregation in sign during worship.

3. Some persons may be uncomfortable learning sign language at first. Consider choosing a familiar song the first time you use sign language with your group. If they already know the text and tune, the participants can concentrate on the sign language itself. They will be able to learn and use it quickly if they are not also trying to remember new words and a new tune.

4. When learning a new song with sign language, consider the following ideas:

- Teach the tune and text first.
- Review the tune and text until the persons are comfortable with them.
- Teach the sign and speak the text in the rhythm of the music.
- Sign and sing together, starting slowly if necessary and gradually increasing to the correct tempo.

5. If a group is leading the sign, help them to do the sign language together. Match the sign to the rhythm of the text and music. Make the motions slower and more graceful to match the mood of the song, if necessary.

6. Finally, encourage persons to simply "try it" when using the sign in congregational worship. It will take repetition to make the combination of text, music, and sign comfortable. Use the same song for several weeks or perhaps over an even longer length of time so that everyone will be able to sign and sing with ease.

Away in a **manger**,   no crib for a **bed**,   the **little Lord Jesus**
(baby)

  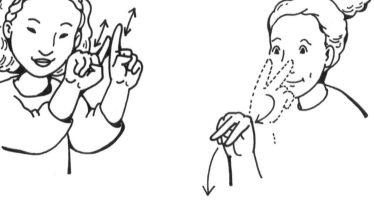

laid down his sweet head.   The **stars** in the sky   **looked down**

 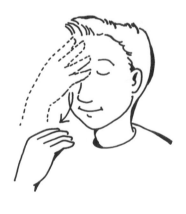

where he lay, the **little Lord Jesus**,   **asleep** on the hay.
(baby)

Away in a Manger

About the Song: Although the stories and legends abound, the one thing we do know about this delightful hymn is that Martin Luther did not write it! The song is presumed to have been written in the United States (not Germany) and first appeared in a Lutheran hymnal that was printed in Philadelphia in 1885. For many years there was also confusion about the composer of the tune. The composer himself referred to Luther when he first published the melody. Recent hymn scholars have attributed the tune to James R. Murray (1887). It is a hymn enjoyed by young and old alike, telling the story of the babe in the manger and asking him to be near us throughout our life.

Performance Options

- Younger children especially enjoy learning the sign to this hymn. Use in choir and educational settings.
- Ask a soloist to sign and sing stanza 1 with the congregation joining in singing stanzas 2 and 3.
- Use this favorite as a part of your Christmas pageant with either a choir or soloist signing and singing.
- If your group enjoys Christmas caroling, consider teaching the sign to the group. Sing this carol at the end of the program at each place you visit and let this become a part of your group's Christmas tradition.
- Add guitar or flute for a simple yet beautiful accompaniment. Consider using a small wind chime to add a light bell sound when using this as an anthem or solo.

WORDS: Anonymous
MUSIC: James R. Murray

This is **my**   story,   this is **my**   song,

praising my Savior all the day long;

(Repeat—same as above.)

This is my story, this is my song, praising my Savior all the day long.

Blessed Assurance
(Refrain)

About the Song: The text to this song was born when Fanny Crosby's friend Phoebe Knapp played the tune once or twice on the piano and asked Fanny what the tune seemed to say to her. Fanny replied "Blessed assurance, Jesus is mine," and the entire text was completed a short time later. Fanny Crosby wrote over eight thousand hymn texts in her lifetime.

Performance Options

- Teach the congregation the sign language and use the refrain as a response to the reading of the Gospel lesson in worship.
- Read the stanzas of the hymn as a litany, with the congregation singing and signing the refrain as a response to each stanza.
- Tell the hymn story or perhaps the story of the life of Fanny Crosby as a part of a devotion for Sunday school, choir, youth group, or any small group meeting. End the devotion by teaching the sign, and then sign and sing the first stanza and refrain.

This is my sto - ry, this is my song,

prais - ing my Sav - ior all the day long;

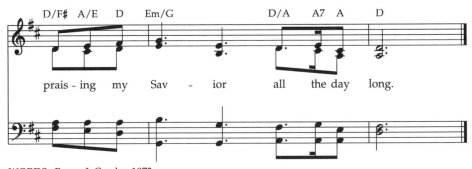

this is my sto - ry, this is my song,

prais - ing my Sav - ior all the day long.

WORDS: Fanny J. Crosby, 1873
MUSIC: Phoebe P. Knapp, 1873

Blessed	be	the	name!			
Blessed	be	the	name!			
Blessed	be	the	name	of	the	Lord!
Blessed	be	the	name!			
Blessed	be	the	name!			
Blessed	be	the	name	of	the	Lord!

Sign Provided: Entire chorus

About the Song: This chorus has a campmeeting origin. It was probably sung between lines of songs or as a refrain for well-known hymns. It is a jubilant praise chorus that reminds us of Psalm 72:19.

Performance Options

- Sing and sign this chorus with the congregation as a part of worship.
- Use this at the close of a Bible study or Sunday school class each week.
- This chorus is very flexible in performance style. Consider adding percussion (drums, tambourine, and so on), guitar, and bass for use as an upbeat praise song. Try singing the chorus unaccompanied with a medium to slow tempo. The use of the sign language in slow, fluid motion can become a beautiful liturgical dance.

Blessed Be the Name

WORDS: USA campmeeting chorus, based on Psalm 72:19
MUSIC: USA campmeeting chorus; arr. Ralph E. Hudson

Come! Come! Everybody worship with a prayer or song of praise!

Come! Come! Everybody worship! Worship God always!

About the Song: Natalie Sleeth was the daughter of musical parents and majored in music theory in college. She married a Methodist clergyman who was a professor. Her first piece of music was published in 1969, and she continued to write and publish music until her death in 1992. Natalie's music continues to be a favorite among children in Sunday school and choir.

Performance Options

- Teach the congregation the sign and use this as a "call to worship."
- Use this as an act of praise with a soloist, choir and congregation. Sing the song three times:
First time: Choir sings and signs the song in English.
Second time: Soloist sings the Spanish text while the choir signs.
Third time: The congregation, choir, and soloist sing and sign together.
- Add simple rhythm instruments played by a children's choir or Sunday school class. Add triangles, finger cymbals, hand drums, and rhythm sticks. Consider these simple patterns or improvise your own:
Hand drum: Play on the first beat of every measure.
Triangles: Play the second half note of every measure.
Finger cymbals: Play on the first beat of measures 1, 3, 5, 7, and 8.
Rhythm sticks: Lightly play quarter notes.

Come! Come! Everybody Worship!
(¡Vengan todos adoremos!)

WORDS: Natalie Sleeth; Spanish trans. Mary Lou Santillán-Baert
MUSIC: Natalie Sleeth
© 1991 Cokesbury

Lord of all,   to   thee   **we raise**
                               (give)

this our **hymn**   of   grateful   **praise**.

Sign Provided: Last line of each stanza

About the Song: The hymn text, a litany of thanksgiving, was inspired by the beautiful countryside near Bath, England. The text reflects the gifts from God that were seen by Pierpoint as he sat looking at the beauty God had created: the beauty of nature that surrounds us, the wonder of God's love, human love, and Jesus.

Performance Options

- Use the hymn text as a litany. The worship leader speaks the text of the first eight measures of a stanza. The congregation responds by singing and signing the last four measures of the stanza.
- Have the choir sing the first three lines of each stanza, with the congregation responding by singing and signing the last line of each stanza.
- Choreograph the hymn for liturgical dance. The congregation joins in the dance as they sign the last four measures of each stanza.

For the Beauty of the Earth

WORDS: Folliot S. Pierpoint
MUSIC: Conrad Kocher

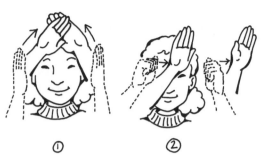 

1. Father, we love you, we **worship** and adore you,

2. Jesus, we love you, we **worship** and adore you,

3. Spirit, we love you, we **worship** and adore you,

glorify thy name in all the earth.
Glorify thy name,
glorify thy name,
glorify thy name in all the earth.

Glorify Thy Name

About the Song: Donna Adkins wrote "Glorify Thy Name" in the summer of 1975. She had been meditating on John 17, in which Jesus prayed not only for his disciples, but also for all who would follow him in years to come. Donna and her husband, Jim, pastor Covenant Church East in Greensburg, Pennsylvania. They have two children and two grandchildren.

Performance Options

- Teach this to the congregation and use it often in a praise medley. The congregation will quickly memorize the text and the song will soon become a part of their praise medley time.
- This is an easily learned song to sing and to sign. Use in Sunday school and confirmation class sessions when you are studying the Trinity.
- Use this as a part of morning and evening devotions on retreats—to begin and end the day "glorifying" the name of God.
- Encourage families to use this in their family devotion time. Even the youngest child can join in the sign language!

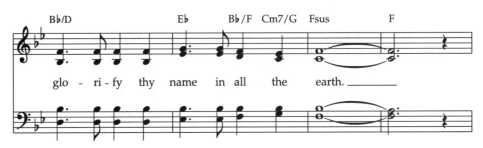

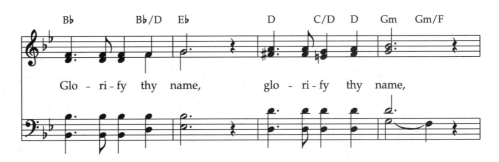

WORDS and MUSIC: Donna Adkins

1.　　God　　is　so　　**good,**
　　　　God　　is　so　　good,
　　　　God　　is　so　　good,
　　　　　　　　he's so **good**　　to　　**me.**

2.　　**God**　　　cares　　　　　　　　for　　me,
　　　　God　　　cares　　　　　　　　for　　me,
　　　　God　　　cares　　　　　　　　for　　me,
　　　　　　　　　　　he's so **good**　to　　**me.**

About the Song: What does it mean when the information given about a song says "traditional"? This means that the song has come from many sources and cannot be attributed to any one composer or author. Often, it is a song that has been taught by one person teaching another and may have been slightly changed as the chain of singers teaching one another gets longer and longer.

Performance Options

- Sing and sign a stanza of the hymn as a response to a time of witness or a time of thanksgiving in worship.
- Younger children's choirs will enjoy leading this song in worship.
- Ask the children to make up more stanzas. Your library will have a sign language reference book to use to learn the sign to the new words. See page 48 for a list of sign language references.
- Use a simple guitar accompaniment with this song or consider singing it SATB, unaccompanied.

God Is So Good

1. God is so good, God is so good,
2. God cares for me, God cares for me,

God is so good, he's so good to me!
God cares for me, he's so good to me!

WORDS and MUSIC: Traditional

He	rose,			
he	rose,			
he	rose	from	the	dead!
He	rose,			
he	rose,			
he	rose	from	the	dead!
He	rose,			
he	rose,			
he	rose	from	the	dead!

and the **Lord**   will   **bear**   my   **spirit**   **home**.
(carry)

Sign Provided: Refrain

About the Song: This African American spiritual tells the story of the last few days of Christ's life and his joyous Resurrection. The stanzas set the scene as we meet Joseph, Mary, and the angel who rolled away the stone from the front of the tomb. The stanzas can be found in several hymnals, including *The United Methodist Hymnal* (#316). We can feel the joy as well as the sorrow of all persons who have heard this story over many generations. Sing this song with exuberance as you join in the procession of believers.

Performance Options

- This joyful spiritual can be used on Easter and during Eastertide as a response to the scripture.
- Once the refrain is well known by the congregation, consider asking a choir to sing the stanzas, with the congregation joining in on the refrain. The stanzas can be found in *The United Methodist Hymnal.*
- If you are unable to sing the men's echo in the refrain, add a tambourine. Play the tambourine in the same rhythm pattern as the men's echo or improvise your own tambourine part.
- Ask several persons to choreograph this hymn to lead the opening procession on Easter Sunday.

He Rose
(Refrain)

WORDS: African American spiritual
MUSIC: African American spiritual; adapt. and arr. William Farley Smith

1. He's got the whole **world** in his **hands**,
   (God)
   he's got the whole **world** in his **hands**,
   he's got the whole **world** in his **hands**,
   he's got the whole **world** in his **hands**.

2. He's got the **wind** and the **rain** in his **hands**,
   he's got the **wind** and the **rain** in his **hands**,
   he's got the **wind** and the **rain** in his **hands**,
   (Repeat last line of stanza 1.)

3. He's got the **sun** and the **moon** in his **hands**,
   he's got the **sun** and the **moon** in his **hands**,
   he's got the **sun** and the **moon** in his **hands**,
   (Repeat last line of stanza 1.)

He's Got the Whole World in His Hands

2. He's got the wind and the rain...
3. He's got the sun and the moon...

WORDS: African American spiritual
MUSIC: African American spiritual; arr. Nylea L. Butler-Moore
Arr. © 1993 Abingdon Press

Sign Provided: Stanza 1 in full, key words in stanzas 2 and 3

About the Song: The African American spiritual is a deeply emotional song that often relates to a biblical passage. In the late nineteenth century, the Jubilee Singers of Fisk University sang concerts across the United States and abroad. Because of their efforts, black spirituals became widely recognized. Spirituals such as "He's Got the Whole World in His Hands" gradually became a part of the song collection of children and adults across the world.

Performance Options

• Ask a soloist to sing this spiritual unaccompanied from a place in the worship space where the congregation cannot see them. Ask a child, youth, or adult who is secure with the sign language to stand in view of the congregation and sign as the soloist sings, to create a dramatic interpretation of the song.

• Memorize the sign language for this spiritual and use it as a part of your lesson any time you need an activity while leading children or youth in class sessions.

• When using this song as a part of a special presentation for preschools, Sunday school, or choir, ask one group to prepare drawings to depict a stanza, ask another to create a dance for another stanza, and another group to learn the sign language to create a variety of visual presentations for the song.

| I | have | **seen,** | I | have | seen | the | Lord! |
| I | have | **seen,** | I | have | seen | the | Lord! |

Sign Provided: Refrain

About the Song: The composer, Dr. James H. Ritchie, Jr., is clergy member of the Western Pennsylvania Annual Conference of The United Methodist Church. Jim is called upon regularly to lead intergenerational experiences and to write or teach in various settings on the subjects of children and worship, music and education, curriculum, and human sexuality education for children. Nylea Butler-Moore, arranger, lives in Santa Clarita, California, where she arranges and composes music for choirs of all ages and for Sunday school.

Performance Options

- Children will enjoy creating choreography to this song. Incorporate the sign language into the choreography.
- Teach the sign language to your congregation and ask your choir or a soloist to sing the stanzas.
- Ask a member who is interested in photography to take pictures that represent the text in the context of your congregation. Show the slides as you sing the song.
- Sing the refrain as a part of worship on the Sundays following Easter to continue the excitement of the first sightings of the resurrected Christ.
- Add percussion, guitar, and bass to make this an upbeat praise song.

I Have Seen

*suggested usage

WORDS: James Ritchie
MUSIC: James Ritchie; arr. Nylea L. Butler-Moore
© 1996 Cokesbury

I love you, Lord, and I lift my voice to worship you.

O my soul   rejoice!   Take joy, my King, in what you hear:

alternating movement

May it be a sweet, sweet sound in your ear.

I Love You, Lord

Sign Provided: Entire song

About the Song: In 1974, Laurie Klein was a young mother and wife living in Oregon. She and her family were barely making it financially and were far away from friends and family. Out of the depth of this time in her life, when she felt most hopeless, came the words and music to this praise song. Since that time Laurie and her husband have raised their two children to adulthood, served on staff at various churches, and continue to write music to praise God.

Performance Options

• Teach this song to the congregation and then add the sign. Use this as a response to a time of confession and forgiveness, at the close of a time of personal witness, or as a part of a celebration of a mission team's work.

• Use the song and sign in Sunday school classes and small group settings as a call to prayer and in the worship time.

• Ask the choir or a vocal soloist to sing the song as a solo dancer combines the sign with liturgical dance.

• Use a simple accompaniment, such as guitar or solo flute.

• Accompany the song with handbells or hand chimes ringing the chords in a simple rhythm pattern.

WORDS and MUSIC: Laurie Klein

How marvelous!

How wonderful!   And   my   song   shall   ever   be:

How marvelous!

How wonderful   is   my   Savior's   love for me!

I Stand Amazed in the Presence

About the Song: In 1905 this text and tune appeared in the collection *Praises.* The text closely follows the story of Christ in the Garden of Gethsemane as found in Luke 22:41-44. This Bible story, a portion of the Passion account, is not found in the other Gospels.

Performance Options

• Teach the sign to the congregation and allow them to enjoy adding movement to this familiar hymn.

• Use the refrain with sign language to affirm one another when something has gone well in rehearsal.

• Use this as part of a group devotion. Read the scripture lesson (Luke 22:41-44) and then ask the group to follow along using the entire hymn text. Sing together the last stanza and refrain, signing the refrain.

• Sing a stanza of the hymn and the refrain as a response to a time of confession or after a profession of faith to echo the personal emphasis of Christ's gift of love to us.

WORDS and MUSIC: Charles H. Gabriel

Yes,	Jesus	loves	me!
Yes,	Jesus	loves	me!
Yes,	Jesus	loves	me!

The **Bible**   tells   me so.

Sign Provided: Refrain

About the Song: The text to this familiar hymn was written into the novel *Say and Seal* by Anna B. Warner in 1860. The stanzas have been revised since that time and many congregations sing selected stanzas that have become part of their local traditions. This hymn became important to the Christian converts living in China during the many years after October 1949 when missionaries were not allowed into the country. In 1972, a simple phrase was added to a message. "The *this I know* people are well!" let us know that the Word was alive in China.

Performance Options
- Sing and sign the song as a response to reading a Bible story about Jesus and his love.
- Children of all ages know this song. Even preschoolers will enjoy signing this song.
- Ask the children to create a rhythm band of homemade instruments to accompany the song in worship as the adults sing and sign.
- Alternate singing the phrases between the men (and boys) and the women (and girls). Everyone joins together to sing and sign the refrain.

Jesus Loves Me

WORDS: Anna B. Warner
MUSIC: William B. Bradbury

Jesus   loves the little **children**, all the children of the **world**.

Red,   brown,   yellow,   black and   white,

they are **precious** in his sight; Jesus   loves the little   **children** of the world.

Jesus Loves the Little Children

About the Song: Did you know that this is the chorus to a hymn of the same title? In 1915, The Heidelberg Press of Philadelphia, Pennsylvania, published a songbook titled *Beginner and Primary Songs for Use in Sunday School and the Home.*

This book would have cost you thirty cents in 1915, but you would get a discount price of twenty-five cents if you ordered multiple copies! According to this songbook, the text was written by Rev. C. H. Woolston, D.D. The hymn begins: "Jesus calls the children dear, 'Come to me and never fear,' " and continues with reminders that Jesus is the Shepherd and he will stand by us. Other stanzas affirm that he is our Savior. The hymn closes with a reminder for us to follow Jesus because of his love for us and for all children everywhere.

Performance Options

- Ask an adult soloist to begin singing the song. Add more and more singers with each person (or group) younger and younger in age until a multigenerational choir is formed. (The reverse will also give the same effect.) Use this song as a gathering song for your intergenerational activities.
- Let the children create their own rhythm band accompaniment to the song. Create a simple ostinato pattern and then encourage the children to take turns signing, singing and improvising the accompaniment.
- Ask your singers to wear solid color T-shirts when they sing this song (red, brown, yellow, and so on). This will create a rainbow of color. Use this song as a theme for a children's celebration day and ask everyone to wear a color of the rainbow to worship.

WORDS: Anonymous
MUSIC: George F. Root

Lord, I lift your **name** on **high;**   Lord, I love to sing your **praises.**

I'm so **glad** you're in my **life;**   I'm so **glad** you came to **save** us,

You came from **heaven** to **earth** to **show** the **way;**

from the **earth** to the **cross,** my **debt** to pay.   From the **cross** to the **grave,**

from the **grave** to the **sky,**   Lord, I lift your **name** on **high.**

32

Sign Provided: Entire song

About the Song: Rick Founds, the composer, has been leading worship since he was fourteen years old. He has written many songs that are used every week in church services across the world. Rick's background is diverse, including music therapy, accounting, welding and machine sciences, and over seventeen years of full-time music ministry. He lives in Southern California.

Performance Options

- Teach the congregation this popular praise song. The addition of the sign language will help them remember the order of the words.
- The addition of drums, guitar, and bass will help keep the tempo moving in an upbeat praise song arrangement.
- Change the mood of the song by asking a soloist to sing and sign the song unaccompanied, in a slower, *legato* style.
- Help your choir learn to read more difficult rhythm patterns by creating several different charts of the rhythm patterns of a variety of the musical phrases in the song. Sixteenth note and dotted eighth/sixteenth note patterns can be learned this way. Upper elementary and middle school choirs will enjoy trying to match your charts to the text.

Lord, I Lift Your Name on High

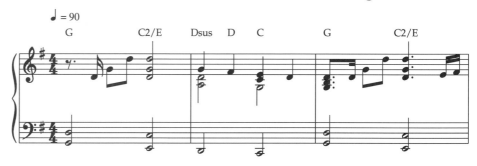

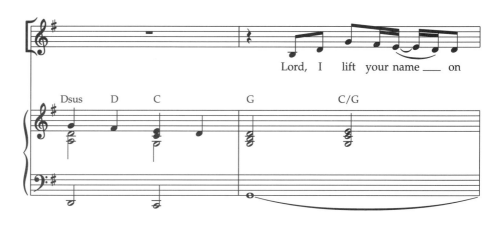

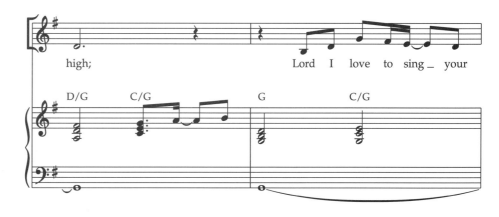

WORDS and MUSIC: Rick Founds

from the grave _ to the sky, _ Lord, I lift your name _ on _

_ high. _

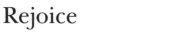

Rejoice　　　　　God's　　　　　people　rejoice!

May I use **words**　to　bring　**peace**　and　**joy**,

as my **God**　　　**requires.**

36

Responses

Sign Provided: Entire response

About the Songs: Why do we sing responses in worship? Worship has been described as a conversation between God and each person. We realize that there are times in worship when we need to say to God "thank you" or "help me." Using sung responses is one way we can do that. Sometimes everyone sings the response; on other occasions it may be sung by a choir or soloist. The composer of these two responses, Joyce Brown, teaches Sunday school and serves as director of the elementary choir at Western Hills UMC in Fort Worth, Texas.

Performance Options

- Use the same response for several weeks. Perhaps you may sing the response during weeks 1 and 2. Then add the sign language during week 3. Sing and sign together week 4 and continuing into the upcoming weeks.
- Use a variety of instruments to accompany the response, such as guitars, flutes, violins, handbells and hand chimes, piano, organ, or electronic keyboard. At times, sing the response *a cappella*. Consider the placement of the response within the worship service and choose the instrumentation according to the style and mood you desire.
- Use one of these short responses in Sunday school or other educational settings as a tool to help focus the students. Sing "Words of Peace" as you move to a time of prayer. "Rejoice, God's People" could be sung and signed at the end of a scripture lesson or at the close of the benediction.
- Sing "Words of Peace" as a part of the choir's prayer prior to leading in worship.

Rejoice, God's People

Re - joice, God's peo - ple, re - joice! _____

WORDS and MUSIC: Joyce Brown
© 1996 Cokesbury

Words of Peace

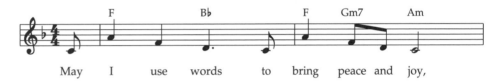

May I use words to bring peace and joy,

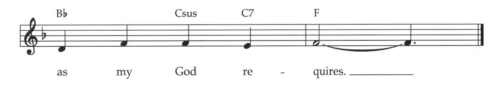

as my God re - quires. _____

WORDS and MUSIC: Joyce Brown
© 1996 Cokesbury

Saints today,
(now)

saints of old,
(past)

known to all by stories told draw us nearer, every nearer.

to the perfect love of God.

Sign Provided: Refrain

About the Song: John Horman wrote this song in memory of a very good friend, John Martin Shepherd. We have come to recognize that a saint is any Christian who has lived their life in a way that has brought someone to a deeper understanding of God. A saint may be someone who lived a long time ago, but a saint can also be a special Sunday school teacher, friend, or family member living today. Mr. Horman lives in Maryland and enjoys writing music that will help the singer and the listener learn more about the Bible and their own faith in God.

Performance Options

- Sing this refrain during a celebration of All Saints Day, or anytime you are exploring the stories of persons who have shown us the way of Christ-like living.

- Teach the sign to the congregation and use the text and sign as a response to the naming of the saints in worship.

- Add handbells or hand chimes to the singing. Have the bell choir ring the chord changes. Another option is to play one of the inner voices of the accompaniment up an octave.

- "Saints Today, Saints of Old" (refrain) is taken from the Abingdon Press anthem of that title written by John D. Horman (Item No. 50161X). Scored for unison children's choir (optional descant), optional SATB choir, and piano, the text recounts the story of saints in the past and reminds us of the saints in our lives today, including teachers, family members, and others. Teach the sign to the congregation and ask them to sign the refrain each time they hear it in the anthem.

Saints Today, Saints of Old
(Refrain)

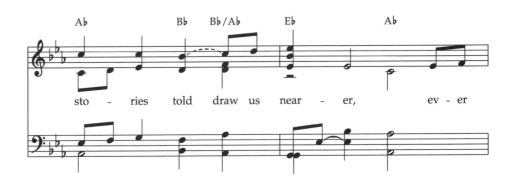

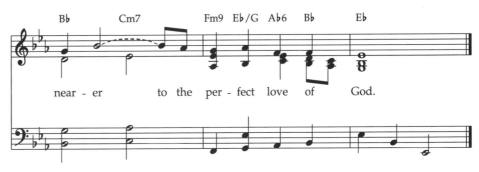

WORDS and MUSIC: John D. Horman
© 1995 Abingdon Press

Shalom to you now, shalom, my **friends.**

May   God's   full mercies **bless** you, my friends.

In all your **living**   and through your **loving,**

Christ   be   your   shalom,
Christ   be   your   shalom.

Shalom to You

About the Song: The Hebrew word *shalom* means both "hello" and "farewell." The text draws us into a prayer for peace, for loving relationships, and for a world where Christ is the center of all of life. The Hispanic tune should be sung reverently and slowly, repeating it as the group desires.

Performance Options

- Use this hymn at the close of worship or any other gathering. If the hymn is not familiar to your congregation, consider teaching only the sign for "shalom" at first. Once they are comfortable with the tune, add more of the sign language.
- A simple accompaniment, such as guitar, is perfect for this hymn. If the guitarist is able, consider asking him or her to play a finger-picked pattern to add a sense of movement to the hymn. Double the melody with recorder or flute as needed.
- Youth and adult choirs will enjoy improvising two-, three-, and four-part choral harmony as they sing. Encourage them to do so as they sign the text.
- Use this as the closing to a long-term Bible study series or other group meeting. Ask the members to sing and sign the hymn once, and then to sing it again as they stand in a circle holding hands.

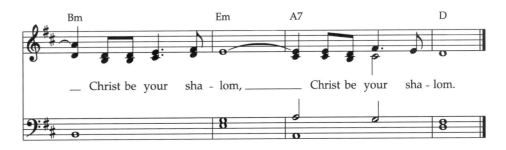

WORDS: Elise S. Eslinger
MUSIC: Traditional Spanish melody; harm. Carlton R. Young

He   is   alive,   yes,   Jesus   is   alive!

Sing   we   the   song   of   victory!

He   is   alive,   yes,

alternating movement

Jesus is alive to   reign   for   eternity!

Sign Provided: *Refrain*

About the Song: Dana Mengel is a freelance composer with over four hundred anthems in print. He lives in Independence, Missouri, with his wife Tammy and their two children, Emmanuel and Gloria. He wrote this piece to be an uplifting part of Easter worship. The refrain repeats the cry "He is alive!" to remind us that Jesus lives again!

Performance Options

- Use this as a choral call to worship on Easter Sunday. Ask the congregation to sing and sign only the phrase "He is alive, yes, Jesus is alive!" The choir would sing the phrases "Sing we a song of victory" and "To reign for eternity!" If you are concerned about trying to learn to sign and sing on Easter Sunday, consider saying the text and signing. Then teach the tune for use during Eastertide.
- Use the text as a speech chorus in Sunday school and encourage the children to improvise an accompaniment using their body (clap, slaps on thighs, stomps, tongue clicks, and so on). Create a "speech and sign" choir and visit another class to share the good news of Christ's Resurrection!
- "Song of Victory" is a refrain created from the anthem of the same name by Dana Mengel. Published by Abingdon Press, it is scored for SATB choir and piano (Item No. 061687). The refrain is sung at the close of each stanza. Perhaps the choir could memorize this triumphant Easter anthem and sing and sign the joyous news of Christ's Resurrection. The handbell part provided with the published anthem setting (measures 1-8) can be played with this refrain.
- Once the congregation has learned this refrain, consider using it at any time during the year when

it is appropriate to affirm that we believe that Christ resurrected!
- Get together a group to go Easter caroling to shut-ins or for a local nursing home. Begin and end your caroling with this refrain. Perhaps the shut-in will be able to join you in the sign! Sing several familiar Easter hymns, such as "Christ the Lord Is Risen Today" or "Low in the Grave He Lay."

Song of Victory
(Refrain)

WORDS and MUSIC: Dana Mengel
© 1996 Abingdon Press

Jesus,   come   teach   us now, come **reach** us now,
(touch)

come **bless**   us   now,   **spreading**   your   love.

About the Song: The composer, Wayne Wold, is an assistant professor of music at Hood College in Frederick, Maryland. He teaches occasional church music topics at Lebanon Valley College in Annville, Pennsylvania, and also directs the choirs and plays organ and piano at Camp David's military chapel on Sundays. It is not uncommon to find the President of the United States in the congregation at Camp David. Wayne wrote the complete anthem because he wanted to help singers think about what it was like to know Jesus when he lived on earth, being able to see his wonderful works, hearing his great words, being taught or healed by Jesus.

Performance Options

- Add flute, recorder, or violin to the accompaniment. Ask the instrumentalist to play the alto line of the piano accompaniment up an octave to easily create an interesting instrumental part.

- Teach the sign to your congregation or choir and use this refrain as a response to the reading of the Gospel lesson, especially during the seasons of the church year when we focus on the ministry of Jesus. Consider adding light tinkling bells, such as wind chimes, for an ethereal sound.

- Once you have taught the sign language to the children in your Sunday school class or choir, add this simple circle dance to your lesson. Ask the children to create two circles, one inside the other. Ask the two circles to move in opposite directions as they sing the first two lines of the music. Stopping at the word "love," the children should turn and face the person in the circle opposite and sign together the last two lines of the refrain. Alternate this refrain and dance with short scripture phrases about Jesus' life and ministry.

- "Spreading Your Love" (refrain) is

Spreading Your Love

WORDS and MUSIC: Wayne L. Wold
© 1994 Abingdon Press

taken from the anthem written by Wayne Wold, and is scored for unison children's choir (optional two-part), handbells (optional), and keyboard. The children's choir would enjoy singing, signing, and ringing this anthem published by Abingdon Press (Item No.

026679). Consider using the refrain for several weeks with the congregation and then plan for the children's choir to sing the anthem. The congregation would easily be able to sing and sign the refrain with the children.

This little   light   of   mine, I'm goin'a let it shine,
This little   light   of   mine, I'm goin'a let it shine;
This little   light   of   mine, I'm goin'a let it shine,
                                                        let it shine,
                                                        let it shine,
                                                        let it shine.

This Little Light of Mine

Sign Provided: Stanza 1 and key words to stanzas 2 and 3

About the Song: The symbol of light was important to the slave poets who sang this song. The text reminds us of the Bible story found in Matthew 5:14-16, but also reflects the prophecy of the light (Christ) that would shine out of the darkness. The tune LATTIMER, written by William Farley Smith, is named after Louis Lattimer. Lattimer, an African American inventor, worked with Thomas Edison and others to develop the incandescent lightbulb.

Performance Options

- This arrangement is meant to be sung expressively. Teach it to your choirs first and they will quickly memorize the text. Add the sign language for a wonderful visual interpretation of the song.
- Many children have learned an upbeat gospel version of this text. Teach them this version so they will be able to consider the text within a different style of music. They will enjoy signing this at the slower tempo. Work together with them to make the sign language movements in unison so that there is no distraction from the beauty of the spiritual.
- This song can be used at any time of the year when you need a time of affirmation of steadfast faith.
- This is especially effective when sung and signed as a part of a candlelit evening service.
- Consider asking a soloist to sing this as the choir signs the text for a unique visual effect of movement to music.
- The songbook *Songs of Zion* includes an SAT choral version of the song (Abingdon Press, 1981).

2. Everywhere I go,   3. All through the night,

WORDS: African American spiritual
MUSIC: African American spiritual; adapt. by William Farley Smith

Additional Resources

Sign Language Resources

Bornstein, Harry and Karen Saulnier. *Signing, Signed English: A Basic Guide.* New York: Crown Publishers, Inc., 1986. A sign language guide using Signed English, which differs slightly from ASL.

Costello, Elaine. *Religious Signing.* New York: Bantam Books, 1986. A collection of signs for words used in religious settings.

Dellinger, Annetta E. *Elizabeth Signs with Love.* St. Louis: Concordia, 1991. A children's storybook using the sign to the song "Jesus Loves Me."

Riekehof, Lottie L. *The Joy of Signing: The Illustrated Guide for Mastering Sign Language and the Manual Alphabet, Second Edition.* Springfield, Mo.: Gospel Publishing House, 1987. A sign language guide using American Sign Language (ASL).

Hymn Story Resources

Adams, Lucy Neeley. *52 Hymn Story Devotions.* Nashville: Abingdon Press, 2000.

Lovelace, Austin C. *Hymn Notes for Church Bulletins.* Chicago: G.I.A. Publications, 1987.

Osbeck, Kenneth W. *101 Hymn Stories.* Grand Rapids: Kregel Publications, 1982.

Sanchez, Diana, ed. *The Hymns of The United Methodist Hymnal.* Nashville: Abingdon Press, 1989.

Young, Carlton R. *Companion to The United Methodist Hymnal.* Nashville: Abingdon Press, 1993.

Alphabetical Index of Hymns and Choruses

Topical Index of Hymns and Choruses